—Collective Biographies—

AMERICAN SPIES AND TRAITORS

Vincent Buranelli

Enslow Publishers, Inc.

40 Industrial Road	PO Box 38
Box 398	Aldershot
Berkeley Heights, NJ 07922	Hants GU12 6BP
USA	UK

http://www.enslow.com

Library of Congress Cataloging-in-Publication Data

Buranelli, Vincent.
    American spies and traitors / Vincent Buranelli.
        p. cm. — (Collective biographies)
    Includes bibliographical references and index.
    ISBN 0-7660-2006-1
    1. Spies—United States—Biography—Juvenile literature. 2.
Traitors—United States—Biography—Juvenile literature. [1. Spies. 2.
Traitors.] I. Title. II. Series.
JK468.I6 B87 2002
327.1273'092'2—dc21
                                        2001006700

Printed in the United States of America

10 9 8 7 6 5 4 3 2 1

To Our Readers: We have done our best to make sure all Internet addresses in this
book were active and appropriate when we went to press. However, the author and the
publisher have no control over and assume no liability for the material available on
those Internet sites or on other Web sites they may link to. Any comments or sugges-
tions can be sent by e-mail to comments@enslow.com or to the address on the back
cover.

Illustration Credits: ArtToday.com: p. 33; Clipart.com: p. 42; Dwight D.
Eisenhower Library: p. 82; Enslow Publishers, Inc.: p. 14; Library of
Congress: pp. 36, 46, 52, 56, 66; National Archives and Records
Administration: pp. 24, 33, 63, 72, 86, 90; National Baseball Hall of Fame
Library, Cooperstown, NY: pp. 94, 98; National Portrait Gallery,
Smithsonian Institution: p. 26; Reproduced from the *Dictionary of American
Portraits*, Published by Dover Publications, Inc., in 1967: p. 16; *The
American Revolution: A Picture Source Book*, Dover Publications, Inc., 1975:
p. 8; The Citadel Archives Museum, Charleston, South Carolina: p. 76.

Cover Illustration: Benedict Arnold: Reproduced from the *Dictionary of
American Portraits*, Published by Dover Publications, Inc., in 1967;
Josephine Baker: National Archives; Moe Berg: National Baseball Hall of
Fame Library, Cooperstown, NY; Belle Boyd: Library of Congress.

Contents

Preface

This is a book about espionage and its use in American history. Espionage is the art and science of spying. From colonial times to the present, there have been many American spies operating at home and abroad. A few stand out for special reasons. They have been interesting personalities, or have been involved in great historical events, or have been the center of dangerous conspiracies. The ten selected for inclusion here were outstanding spies.

They were either famous or infamous. For Americans, the famous are those who spied for America and were therefore patriots. The infamous spied against America and were therefore called traitors. These two types appeared as early as the American Revolution. Nathan Hale was a spy and a patriot. Benedict Arnold was a spy and a traitor. Patience Wright was a spy and a patriot in London.

The Civil War created a division between the American people, North and South, and also between the spies of the conflict. Rose Greenhow and Belle Boyd spied for the South against the North. They were considered patriots in the South and traitors in the North. Elizabeth Van Lew spied for the North against the South. She was considered a patriot in the North and a traitor in the South.

Allan Pinkerton has a special place in our list of American spies. He was an immigrant, born in Scotland. He first became a spy in America during the Civil War. Later, he created a network of spies and became a spymaster.

World War II produced remarkably different spies. Many came from unrelated backgrounds. Mark Clark was a general in the United States Army. Josephine Baker was an American actress living in France. Moe Berg was a baseball player. Clark was in the American invasion of North Africa. Baker was in Paris when the Germans invaded and conquered France. Berg was traveling with a team of American baseball players in Japan when America needed a spy in Tokyo. Clark, Baker, and Berg were in the right place at the right time to become spies.

These ten spies lived in different centuries, from the American Revolution to World War II. Five of the ten, Wright, Greenhow, Boyd, Van Lew, and Baker, were women. One, Baker, was African American. Of the five men, four were patriots, Hale, Pinkerton, Clark, and Berg. One, Arnold, was a traitor, and he remains the most infamous American traitor of all.

Much about American espionage can be learned from studying the spy careers of these ten men and women. So can much about American history.

Nathan Hale

George Washington's Spy

Nathan Hale would probably never have become a spy if the American Revolution had not broken out in 1775. He was a teacher in New London, Connecticut, when news arrived that colonial minutemen had clashed with British soldiers at Lexington and Concord. They were called minutemen because they were ready to fight "at a minute's notice." Like many other patriots, Hale joined up to fight for the Americans against the British.

A town meeting was held in New London to discuss the crisis. Hale spoke up boldly for more just resistance to tyranny. He was reported to have urged his fellow townsmen forward with the words: "Let us

American spy Nathan Hale was captured by the British and executed
on September 22, 1776.

march immediately and never lay down our arms until we obtain our independence."[1]

This was a bold thing to say because Americans were divided about how far to go in resisting King George III of England. Some simply wanted to end the taxes imposed on them by the king and the British Parliament. Others were for dividing power between the colonies and the mother country. The radicals were those who demanded complete freedom for America. Hale agreed with the radicals. He chose the winning side as the colonies marched from resistance to independence.

The colonials besieged the British in Boston. The Second Continental Congress, the new government of the colonies, named George Washington to command the colonial army. The battle of Bunker Hill was fought in June 1775. Washington arrived to take command and drew up the plan that forced the British to evacuate Boston.

Nathan Hale was there when the king's soldiers went aboard their troop ships and sailed away to Nova Scotia. This was where the British gathered their forces and planned their attacks.

Hale was a soldier. He was not yet a spy. Ironically, he could have met a spy operating in Washington's headquarters outside Boston. Dr. Benjamin Church was surgeon general of the American army and therefore had access to military information. A secret loyalist, meaning loyal to the king of England, Church sent undercover agents to carry into Boston reports in code about Washington's military strength, available supplies, and weapons. One of Church's agents was caught. The agent confessed, and Church was exposed, ending his anti-American espionage.[2]

Nathan Hale was born in Coventry, Connecticut, on June 6, 1755. He was the sixth child of Richard Hale and Elizabeth Strong, who owned a successful farm in Coventry. He grew up on the farm, and attended an elementary school in Coventry.

At home, he read the Bible with his family and thought of becoming a minister. After high school, he went to Yale University, where he studied Latin and decided to become a teacher. In 1774, he began to teach at the Union Grammar School in New London, Connecticut. Union Grammar was a boys' school, but Hale persuaded the director to let him teach a class of girls. Hale's move was an advance in education for the time. He was one of the few educators in New London who considered the education of girls to be as important as the education of boys.[3]

In 1775, the American Revolution began. Hale enlisted in the Seventh Connecticut Regiment, rising to the rank of captain.

General George Washington, the commander of the colonial army, ordered the Seventh to the siege of Boston. Hale took part in the military maneuver when Washington lined up his artillery on Dorchester Heights overlooking the city. The guns pointing down at him forced General William

Howe, the British commander, to retreat from Boston on March 17, 1776.

Washington believed that Howe would return to attack, this time with New York as his military target. If he seized the Hudson River, it would split the northern colonies from the southern ones. The American commander therefore moved his troops from Boston to Long Island off New York City to challenge the attack.

The challenge failed. Howe and the British troops defeated the Americans on Long Island. Washington, to avoid being surrounded, ordered his army to cross over to New York City.[4]

At this moment, Hale proved to be an excellent leader. He led his company in an attack under the guns of an enemy ship, set it ablaze, and made off with a number of its cannons. The operation was so daring and so successful that Washington expressed his gratitude to the men who carried it through.[5]

One of Washington's hardest problems was that he could not tell what Howe was planning. Howe had the ability to move against him from different directions. Washington agonized over his ability to arrange his defenses to meet the coming attack.

On September 2, 1776, he wrote to the Continental Congress about his lack of an effective intelligence system. Four days later he returned to this vital subject: "We have not been able to obtain the least information as to the enemy's plans."[6]

Washington ordered Colonel Thomas Knowlton to find a man brave enough to become a spy. Knowlton called his officers and asked for a volunteer. Not one responded until the youngest of Knowlton's captains spoke up, saying he would accept the assignment. The captain was Nathan Hale. A friend tried to argue Hale out of it. This friend stressed the perils of espionage, such as capture. That would leave him facing execution. Hale would not be frightened. He resolved to go, and he went.[7]

The first difficulty was to get behind the enemy lines without arousing suspicion. Hale took a roundabout route. He went to Stamford, Connecticut, where he removed his military uniform and put on civilian clothes. If stopped and questioned by British soldiers, his cover story would be that he was a teacher looking for a job. He took his Yale diploma with him, intending to show it to support his story.[8]

Hale was ferried by a patriot boatman to Long Island, where he made his way inland from the shore and began his espionage. It is impossible to trace his movements precisely. There was no point in remaining on Long Island because the theater of war shifted to New York City. Needing to maintain contact with the enemy forces, Hale followed the British crossing.

Hale slipped in among Howe's forces, recording in his notes everything he thought would be helpful for Washington to know. His mission was to observe how their offensive against the Americans was being prepared. We can assume that he covered British military regiments, their arms, their provisions, their horses, and their transportation wagons. He knew that the British Army was stronger than the American army. It was vital for him to report the facts as he saw them. Underestimating the enemy might be fatal.

Hale wrote in Latin, no doubt hoping the classical language could not be read by anyone who might challenge him.[9] He placed his notes in his shoes, where they were bound to raise suspicion if discovered. But then, he believed he could pass through the British lines and safely reach the American lines. He took too lightly the threat caused by New York's divided population. Both patriots and loyalists lived in the city, and there were many who pretended to be on one side or the other. He could not always tell whether a man or woman he was speaking to could be trusted. His overconfidence proved to be his downfall.

Hale's espionage career was a short one, lasting less than two weeks. How and why his disguise was penetrated remains a mystery. It was rumored at the time that he talked about his spy mission to a person pretending to be a patriot. The person then warned the British authorities that Hale was a spy in their midst. The only known facts are that he was arrested and searched. The incriminating notes were found in his shoes. They were read, perhaps by a British chaplain who knew Latin. They proved he was a spy for Washington.

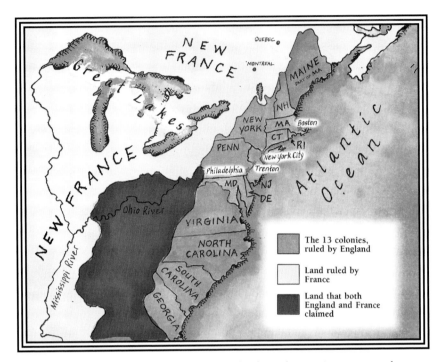

Before the American revolution, much of North America was owned by England and by France.

What we hear of the events that followed came from the British officers holding him. They considered him an officer and a gentleman, like themselves, even if he was their enemy. They respected his coolness in the face of death.

Hale made no attempt to lie about his activities on Long Island and in New York City. He confessed that he was behind the British lines on an espionage mission. He accepted without protest the death sentence imposed on him, which he knew was in accordance with the laws of war. General Howe would not allow a court-martial to render a verdict. He ordered the prisoner to be executed the following day.

Everything we know indicates that Hale spent a tranquil night in meditation. In the morning he is said to have written two letters, apparently one to Colonel Knowlton, the other to his brother, Enoch Hale, who would spy on the British himself after they returned to New York in 1778. No one can be sure because the letters were destroyed by British Provost Marshal William Cunningham, who had charge of the execution.[10]

Hale asked for a Bible to read before being led to the gallows. Cunningham refused. Hale was marched to an apple tree, where a hangman's noose dangled from one limb. At the last moment, the condemned man asked to be permitted to speak to a clergyman. This request, too, was denied. Ever since, the conduct of the provost marshal has been regarded as indefensible.

Hale was hanged on September 22, 1776. His reported last words have remained inspiring to this day. "I only regret that I have but one life to lose for my country."

Benedict Arnold

Benedict Arnold
Patriot, Spy, and Traitor

In the summer of 1777, the Revolutionary War was being fought between the Americans and the British. The two armies marched along the banks of New York's Hudson River. The prize for which they were preparing to fight was the city of Albany, about 130 miles north of New York City. Albany was a military strong point. In New York, the American Revolution was a struggle for the river. Whoever held Albany dominated the Hudson.

For the British, that would split the colonies, north from south. Cooperation would be cut off between the two centers of rebellion: Boston, Massachusetts, and Philadelphia, Pennsylvania. The Americans were determined to prevent the capture of Albany, their key city on the Hudson.

British General John Burgoyne led his troops south from Canada, past Lake Champlain, and reached the Hudson. He drove toward Albany. American General Horatio Gates drew up his forces in front of Albany. He was ready to challenge Burgoyne in a showdown.

Serving under Gates was one of America's most trusted military commanders, General Benedict Arnold.

The two armies, British and American, clashed near Saratoga, New York, on September 19, 1777, and the battle continued until October 13. Arnold was in the heat of the battle. He rode his horse between the battle lines, waving his sword, inspiring his men to stand fast. "Come on, brave boys, come on!" he shouted.[1] His leadership encouraged the Americans to charge forward and force the enemy back. Burgoyne tried to regroup his army and continue fighting, but Arnold led a series of attacks that made this impossible. Surrounded, Burgoyne surrendered to the Americans.

Arnold was the hero of the Battle of Saratoga. He stayed in the fighting to the end, until a bullet hit him in the leg. The wound was so severe that he had to be carried from the battlefield. He walked with a limp for the rest of his life and was never able to take part in another battle.

If Arnold had been killed in the Battle of Saratoga, he would be remembered as a patriot. Instead, he is remembered as a spy and traitor.

Benedict Arnold was born on January 14, 1741, in Norwich, Connecticut. His father was a businessman who failed in business, became an alcoholic, and left his family in debt. Arnold's mother read her Bible and took care of her children by herself. There was no money to send Benedict to college. After his schooling, she placed him with a druggist to learn the craft of making pills and delivering them to the sick. He learned so well that he became a druggist himself.

He ceased to be a druggist in 1775 with the outbreak of the American Revolution. He signed up to fight with the American forces against the British forces of King George III. He soon showed that he was a military genius.

Arnold planned and helped lead the assault that captured Ticonderoga, the British fort on Lake Champlain in northern New York. He led an invasion of Canada in an attempt to capture Quebec. The attempt failed, but the winter trek through eight hundred miles of wilderness was a great achievement.[2] He then went to Lake Champlain, where he gathered enough boats to make a small navy. His ships stopped a British force trying to cross the lake from Canada and retake Ticonderoga.

Then came the climax—the Battle of Saratoga. After Arnold's heroics in the victory, Washington rewarded him by giving him control of Philadelphia. Washington chose a city command because Arnold's Saratoga injury made it impossible for him to return to the battlefield. Arnold entered Philadelphia on

June 19, 1778, and the people turned out by the thousands to cheer the hero of Saratoga.

Arnold seemed to have a post made to order for him in Philadelphia. Yet, he turned traitor and betrayed the American cause.

Arnold did it because the Continental Congress refused to give him a promotion in the army. He was accused of taking part in dishonest business deals. He denied the charge, but the verdict went against him.[3] He felt insulted after all he had done for the Americans on the battlefield. Besides, he owed a lot of debts. He needed the increased pay a military promotion would have brought him.

Arnold had a violent temper. He resented his treatment by his superiors, including Washington. He decided that the American Revolution was a mistake because the British were bound to win the war. His wife, Peggy Shippen, was a loyalist who supported King George III. She urged Arnold to switch sides, which he did. He now supported the British against the Americans.[4]

While he was in Philadelphia, Arnold sent secret messages to the British commander in New York, General Henry Clinton. Arnold became a spy for Clinton, reporting on Washington's plans for the war and on the condition of Washington's army. In return, Arnold asked for a large sum of money and a high command in the British Army. The stage was set for the worst betrayal in American history when

Washington gave Arnold command of West Point in New York on the Hudson.

West Point today is the home of the United States Military Academy, which was founded after the American Revolution. During the American Revolution, it was a fort between New York City and Albany. British General Clinton, in New York City, wanted to move his forces up the river and capture West Point. Washington wanted to hold West Point at all costs. On August 3, 1780, Washington gave command of the fort to Arnold. He trusted Arnold to defend West Point against any British attacks. Arnold drew up a defense plan, which Washington approved.[5]

Arnold lied to Washington. He had no intention of defending West Point. On the contrary, he was in a plot to commit treason by surrendering West Point to the British as soon as they appeared up the Hudson. Arnold pointed out to Clinton in his secret messages that he could now offer West Point as part of the bargain. In return, Arnold demanded twenty thousand pounds and the rank of general in the British Army.

Clinton agreed to Arnold's terms. He ordered John André, his espionage chief, to meet Arnold secretly behind the American lines. They would discuss details of the plot to surrender West Point. Clinton ordered André to stay in uniform so that the Americans could not call him a spy. If he changed into civilian clothes, he would be trying to hide among the American people. If caught, he could be executed as a spy.

Arnold and André met at Haverstraw on the west bank of the Hudson on September 21, 1780. Arnold, as an American general, moved freely from West Point down the river to the meeting. André, a British officer, had to move secretly up the river from New York City. He went on a British boat named the *Vulture*, which slipped past the American defenses and landed him at Haverstraw. He told the *Vulture's* captain to wait for him.

It was past midnight when André arrived. Arnold was waiting for him. They discussed details about how Arnold could surrender West Point by weakening its defenses. Arnold gave André a map of the fort to guide a British attack.

Arnold went back to West Point. However, André could not return to the *Vulture* because American guns fired on the boat, forcing it to retire down the Hudson. André had to find another way to get back to New York City. Arnold had given him a pass through the American lines under the name "John Anderson." André therefore believed it was safe for him to go by land, down the banks of the river.

André made one fatal mistake. He disobeyed Clinton's order to stay in uniform. He changed into civilian clothes, thinking they would conceal the fact that he was a British officer. The civilian clothes made him a spy.[6]

André crossed the Hudson and rode horseback down the east bank of the river toward the British lines near New York City. He almost made it when he reached Tarrytown, where he was stopped by American sentries. André told them his name was John Anderson and showed them the pass given to him by Arnold. At first the Americans believed André. Then the truth came out because the map of West Point was found in his boot.

The Americans sent a report to the commanding general at West Point, Benedict Arnold. Knowing the plot to surrender West Point had failed, Arnold fled to the *Vulture* on the Hudson. He was taken down to New York City.

Word that a British spy had been caught by American sentries was also sent to Washington, who was on his way to West Point to visit Arnold. Washington was amazed to find that Arnold had disappeared. After questioning the men on duty there, Washington realized that Arnold had gone over to the enemy.[7] Arnold was a traitor, and he had escaped.

André was not so lucky. He was held for trial as a spy. André was a captive of the Americans and Arnold was a refugee with the British, so could there not be an exchange of André for Arnold? Washington proposed such an exchange, but Clinton refused.[8] So, Arnold got away while André was eventually executed.

In New York City, Clinton made Arnold a general, and permitted him to lead raids against the

The Unfortunate DEATH of MAJOR ANDRE

(Adjutant General to the English Army) at Head Quarters in New York, Oct.ʳ 2. 1780, who was found within the American Lines in the character of a Spy.

Englishman John André was found guilty of spying in his scheme with Benedict Arnold. While Arnold got away, André was executed.

Americans in Virginia and Connecticut. The raids were too small to have any effect on the war. All Arnold did was to show his bitterness toward the patriots. He had once been one of them. Now he hated them.

Arnold paid a high price for his treason. He did not receive the welcome he expected in New York City. Most of the British disliked him personally. The officers in Clinton's army despised him for committing treason, even though he was on their side. They knew he had broken his word to Washington and was therefore guilty of disloyalty. They also hated Arnold for leaving André to his fate. They thought that Arnold and André should have faced the spy trial together.[9]

Arnold was demoralized by the British defeat in the American Revolution. He could not bear the thought of Washington as the winning general, or as president of the United States.

Arnold went to England with his wife and children.[10] Turning to business, he became the owner of ships trading with Canada and the West Indies. His trading ventures failed, and he fell into poverty. He was an outcast when he died in London on June 14, 1801.[11]

Patience Wright

Patience Wright
Patriot Spy in London

Patience Wright was an American artist who sailed to London in 1772 hoping to make a career for herself. The British capital was a bustling city of more than half a million people.[1] The center of an empire, it benefited from overseas trade with the colonies. Upper-class men and women had money to spend, and many paid artists to represent them in paint and stone.

Wax was another medium used for busts and statues. Patience Wright worked in wax, using a technique she invented.[2] She used to hold a block of wax under her apron to keep it warm and pliable. In cold weather she sat next to the fire in the grate. Her fingers nimbly molded the features of the person opposite her. At the end, she whipped the wax figure from under her apron and added details like eye color. Then she presented the figure to her model.

Many sitters testified that her difficult technique worked beautifully, representing them in a lifelike way. Her fame spread. More and more Londoners came to the Wright studio to be molded in wax. She was invited to the royal palace by King George III and Queen Charlotte.

Her customers included members of Parliament, gentlemen who owned country estates, merchants rich from trade, and military men renowned for the battles they won.

A catalogue of Wright's waxworks reveals that she had at least fifty and perhaps a hundred sitters, some of whom she modeled more than once.[3] She eclipsed all rivals who worked in wax in London. She had made a successful career for herself—the one she had come looking for.

When the American Revolution began in 1775, Wright was a popular American in London. She was also an American spy.

Patience Wright was born in 1725 on a farm in Bordentown, New Jersey. She was a daughter of John Lovell and Patience Townsend, both descendants from English settlers in America. They had ten children, two of whom, Patience and Rachel, had artistic talent.

The Lovell family were Quakers. They believed in the Inner Light, or divine guidance that reveals religious truths to all believers. One such truth was pacifism, the duty to avoid violence. This meant that Quakers should never support a war on either side. Violence toward animals was also forbidden. The Lovells were therefore vegetarians.

Patience grew up in this Quaker tradition. However, she was strong-minded and thought for herself. She abandoned pacifism when she saw freedom being attacked. So, she supported the American Revolution when it came. She was a patriot from start to finish.

As a child she showed artistic ability. She began modeling in clay, which she abandoned in favor of wax. She continued with wax until she was twenty-three. Then she married Joseph Wright. Her interest was now in her family rather than her art.

In 1769, her husband died, leaving her with five children to support. She did this by becoming a professional sculptor in wax. It has been said that she started in America the kind of wax museums we now have.[4]

However, colonial America did not offer Wright enough business for the success she wanted. At that time, London was a much better place to try. So, she crossed the Atlantic and settled in the British capital. Here, she found a bigger population interested in her waxworks.

She had more customers with more money. Soon she was making a good living.

In the year of her arrival, 1772, resistance to British rule was boiling up in the thirteen colonies. Wright threw her support to the resistance. Two years later, she began to spy for the Americans. She was able to do this because of information British leaders revealed as they sat for her to have their images set in wax. They chatted about their government's plans for the colonies, including war if necessary.

Wright cleverly let them talk as if what they said meant nothing to her. Then she reported what she heard to Americans she knew in London. She also wrote to the colonial government, the Continental Congress, in Philadelphia.

Wright was surprised when fighting broke out in 1775 in the battles of Lexington and Concord. She expanded her spy operations into an espionage system with many secret agents. She often used her secret agents to carry her reports to Americans in London. She also had British supporters who knew what she was doing. They backed the colonies. They too, opposed the king. They wanted democratic freedoms for themselves.

Wright moved around London, listening to what was being said about the American crisis. Once she went to Parliament, the center of British politics, and sat in the gallery when the Boston Tea Party was being discussed. She heard the king's ministers debate harsh measures to put down the rebellion in Boston, where, in 1773, a group of citizens hurled crates of tea into the harbor rather than pay the tea tax.

Wright got away with her spying, because the British authorities never suspected her. To them, she was simply a Quaker lady pursuing her profession of wax sculptor. She encouraged this belief by using Quaker language. She said "thee" instead of "you." She addressed people by their first names, even the king and queen. To her, they were "George" and "Charlotte."[5] She refused to curtsy to them as all other women did.

The royal couple could have ordered her to behave herself when she was with them in the palace. Instead, they were amused by her Quaker manners.

Much of her conversation had little to do with spying. Captain Philip Thicknesse, a British soldier, mentioned that she was talkative with him about her early life.[6] She described her parents, her siblings, and the Quaker principles that guided the family. She let it be known that she was pro-American. This was safe since many in London did the same. Espionage was another matter, and she concealed the fact that she was a spy.

Consequently, Wright was allowed to go her way in London. She used this freedom to gather secrets about political and military matters.

She chatted with Lord North, the British prime minister, as he sat for her. North was responsible for the laws that made the American Revolution inevitable. These were especially the taxes that caused the American outcry, "Taxation without representation is tyranny!" Lord North talked freely with Wright, whom he presumed to be of the king's party. He never suspected that in telling her his plans, he was also telling the colonial rebels across the Atlantic in America.

She also talked with Lord Chatham, the former British prime minister, who was pro-American. These meetings in her studio enabled her to tell the Continental Congress in 1774 that North was a die-hard enemy. She added that "Lord Chatham is your friend."[7]

The year 1775 was an important one in which Wright learned about new plans for the British military. In March, she wrote to Benjamin Franklin, who was in London representing the colonies. She warned him that Parliament approved of the British Navy seizing American ships on the high seas. In April, she reported that the British Army was being armed with a new type of artillery "portable on horseback."

Wright was not perfect. One mistake she made was when she reported that General William Howe, the British military commander, was on his way to America. "Howe," she wrote, "is to land at New York."[8] However, Howe had sailed for Boston.

The confused situation in London meant that false reports were inevitable. She might have misunderstood what was being said by politicians. Or, her informants might have misunderstood. They might have rushed to be first with the news instead of waiting to be certain of the facts. Nevertheless, most of Wright's reports were reliable. She was accurate most of the time.

Wright was gratified by the Declaration of Independence on July 4, 1776, and by the American victory at Yorktown in 1781. The climax came when King George III ordered his government to recognize the right of Americans to govern themselves.

Benjamin Franklin   King George III

The tensions of the war years were over. Americans and their supporters in London could now speak freely and without fear. Wright was one of them. She met with friends who had agreed with her during the struggle. She was greeted by former opponents who accepted the triumph of the colonials. Even members of the nobility came to her studio to celebrate American independence with her. She wrote to Benjamin Franklin in Paris in 1783: "I am now in fashion."[9]

At that time, she sent a personal letter to George Washington at his home in Mount Vernon, Virginia. She expressed a hope that she might one day model America's hero in wax. Washington replied that he would be "proud" to sit for her if she returned to America.[10] That never happened, but she cherished his letter. She kept it in her files, where it was found after her death.

Although her days of espionage were finished, Wright continued to watch what was going on in London. She still had an interest in the fate of the British government. She hoped that George III would be compelled to quit because of the British defeat in America. Her desire at that point was to have the British people saved from his tyranny. She looked to a new dawn of freedom on both sides of the Atlantic. This was a vain hope. George III survived the loss of the American colonies and sat on his throne until his death in 1815.

Meanwhile, Wright was growing old. Her health was failing. She had to give up wax modeling, and she spent her time reading or writing letters. Appropriately, her last visit was to that symbol of the new American nation, its London embassy, where she talked with Ambassador John Adams. She collapsed on her return home and died at the age of sixty-one. She left letters about her days as a spy that justified her saying to Franklin: "Women are always useful in great events."[11]

This print of Rose Greenhow with her daughter, Rose, at Washington's Old Capitol prison was taken by Alexander Gardner in 1862. Gardner was one of Mathew Brady's photographers.

Rose Greenhow

Confederate Spy in Washington

In the year 1860, Washington, D.C., was a tense city. This was the period just before the Civil War. Northerners and Southerners were quarreling over whether any state had a right to secede from the Union. Could some of them, it was asked, set up a new nation of their own? The Northerners said that no such right existed and that the Union must be preserved. The Southerners insisted that they had a right to secede from the United States and would do so if the North pushed them too far.

Many on both sides gathered at the home of Rose Greenhow. They came because Greenhow threw the best parties in Washington. She owned a big house where she could entertain dozens of guests at the same time. At the top of her guest list was President

James Buchanan, who was a Northerner defending the American Union. On the other hand, she also invited Senator Jefferson Davis of Mississippi, who would be elected president of the Southern Confederacy after the Southern states seceded.[1]

Greenhow sent invitations to members of Congress on both sides. She welcomed military men of the army and the navy. Some would fight for the North in the Civil War and others for the South. In short, she invited all who could help her understand the quarrel between the states.

Greenhow favored the South. She wanted to talk to Southerners to see what they intended to do if rebellion came. She would then support them as much as she could. At the same time, she wanted to talk to Northerners to find out their plans if a rebellion started. Her purpose was to reveal those plans to the Southerners.

So, Greenhow cultivated both sides, gathered information from both, and kept a record of what they told her. The important thing is that she reported what she knew to her Southern friends. She concealed what she knew from her Northern friends.

She kept this up after Abraham Lincoln, a Northerner, was elected president in 1860 with a pledge to save the Union. The Southern Confederacy declared its independence. The Civil War began. Greenhow was still in Washington. She became a spy for the Confederacy while living in Washington during the Civil War.

Rose O'Neale Greenhow was born in 1817 in Montgomery County, Maryland. Her father was John O'Neale, a planter who raised and sold tobacco. Her mother belonged to a farming family. Rose therefore grew up in the country where she learned to love nature. Her father died when she was just an infant.

At sixteen, Rose was sent with her two sisters to live with an aunt who ran a boardinghouse in Washington, D.C.[2] A boardinghouse is a place where the owner rents rooms to men and women. Here Rose moved into a wider world than Montgomery County. Washington was the capital of the United States, and therefore the center of power for the entire nation.

Many different types of people paid to stay at the boardinghouse. These types were being narrowed down to just two—pro-slavery and antislavery. During Rose's years in the boardinghouse, the pro-slavery became Confederates, and the antislavery became Unionists. These were the sides that clashed in the Civil War.

In 1835, Rose O'Neale married Robert Greenhow. It was in their big house that she became a Washington hostess favoring the South against the North. She and her husband had four daughters before he died in 1854.

In 1859, an event occurred that made her more pro-Southern than ever. Antislavery activist John Brown led an attempt to start a slave revolt at

Harpers Ferry, Virginia. The revolt failed, and Brown was captured and executed.

Greenhow took Brown's attempted revolt as a warning that the South should prepare for war.[3] She spoke to Northerners about the plans being discussed in the White House and in Congress. They did not realize that she passed the information to her friends from the South. Living in the North, she was building a network of spies against the North.

Her espionage activities moved into high gear when Abraham Lincoln was elected president in 1860. This led to the outbreak of the Civil War in 1861. Southerners left the United States armed forces and returned home to fight for their states. One was Lieutenant Thomas Jordan of Virginia, who became an espionage officer of the Confederacy. Knowing Greenhow intended to stay in Washington, Jordan asked her to keep spying and report to him when she could. Greenhow agreed to do this.

The Union generals wanted to capture Richmond, Virginia, the capital of the Confederacy. Richmond was only about one hundred miles from Washington, but in front of the city lay a strong point that had to be taken first. The strong point was called Bull Run by the Unionists and Manassas by the Confederates. Bull Run, a small stream, flowed through the area. The Manassas Railroad could bring more Confederate troops from the west. The Union plan was to seize the railroad and prevent

Confederate reinforcements from getting to the battlefield.

Greenhow knew so much about Union strategy that she must have had an informant in the high command of the United States Army. She used secret agents to deliver her messages to the Confederates.

One agent was Betty Duvall, who took Greenhow's first important message about the Battle of Bull Run.[4] On July 10, 1861, Duvall disguised herself as a farm girl taking her wagon to market. She drove her horse through the Union line where no soldier suspected that a farm girl might be a spy. She delivered her message from Greenhow regarding Union General Irvin McDowell. It read: "McDowell has certainly been ordered to advance on the sixteenth."[5]

The message was so important that Thomas Jordan, now handling Confederate espionage, sent a secret agent to Greenhow asking for more. On July 15, Greenhow sent him her second message, reading: "McDowell, with 35,000 men, will advance this day from Arlington Heights and Alexandria on to Manassas via Fairfax Court House and Centreville."[6]

On July 17, Greenhow sent her third message: a warning that McDowell ordered his forces to capture the railroad at Manassas in order to prevent Confederate reinforcements from joining Confederate General Pierre Beauregard at Bull Run.[7]

Greenhow was a successful spy when she reported on Union forces at Bull Run. Within a week, she

Information supplied by Greenhow allowed Confederate troops to turn the Battle of Bull Run into a rout.

revealed the size of McDowell's army, his line of march, and his plan to cut the Manassas Railroad. All this was known to Beauregard as he arranged his defenses. He saved the railroad and allowed ten thousand men to join him in the battle.

General Thomas J. Jackson held his ground for the Confederates. This was how he earned his nickname "Stonewall" Jackson. The Confederates turned the Battle of Bull Run into a rout.

However, Greenhow's activities caused her to be suspected of spying. Union spymaster in Washington, Allan Pinkerton, ordered his men to watch her house.[8] They saw secret agents going in and coming out. They invaded her house and took it over. They found evidence against her in the form of her letters, notes, and secret messages to the Confederates.

Pinkerton made Greenhow a prisoner in her own house. Her servants were held as well. On January 18, 1862, Pinkerton had her arrested and held for trial on spy charges. Greenhow and her young daughter, Rose, were sent to Washington's Old Capitol Prison. The verdict of the court was announced four months later. Greenhow was found guilty of spying against the United States. The penalty for spying was death. Greenhow received a milder sentence. The court ordered her to leave Washington, to go to the Confederacy, and to stay there.

Greenhow went to Richmond because it was the capital of the Confederacy. She received a warm welcome from Southerners who knew how she had spied for them in Washington. President Jefferson Davis said to her: "But for you there would have been no Battle of Bull Run."[9]

Greenhow was in Richmond when the South won brilliant victories over the North. The greatest of these was at Chancellorsville in Virginia's Shenandoah Valley. Still, Stonewall Jackson was killed accidentally by his own men, a tragedy from which the South never recovered. The tide turned against the Confederacy.

Attempting to prevent defeat, Greenhow agreed to go to Europe for aid. She went to Paris and London, where she defended the cause of the South to everyone who would listen.[10] It did no good. The Confederacy received no help from abroad, and it became steadily weaker.

One thing Greenhow did in London was to publish *My Imprisonment and the First Year of Abolition Rule at Washington*. The word "abolition" meant slavery was abolished, ended. This followed Lincoln's Emancipation Proclamation. In her book, Greenhow claimed the South was justified in fighting for slavery and states' rights.[11]

On August 10, 1864, Greenhow sailed from England for America aboard the *Condor*. Her ship ran into a Union blockade of the southern coast. The captain was unable to land, so Greenhow demanded to be rowed ashore in a lifeboat. A violent storm arose and overturned the lifeboat. Greenhow drowned in heavy surf.

Her funeral service was held in Wilmington, North Carolina. Those who admired her as a Confederate spy in Washington draped a Confederate flag over her coffin.[12]

Greenhow did not live to know that her excellent spy work did not bring victory to the Confederacy. She never heard of the Confederate surrender in 1865. She never knew the South lost the Civil War.

Elizabeth Van Lew

Elizabeth Van Lew
Union Spy in Richmond

Elizabeth Van Lew of Richmond, Virginia, had a nickname. They called her "Crazy Bet" because of her odd behavior. She stumbled from side to side as she walked along the streets of Richmond. She mumbled to herself and sang songs in a loud voice. She talked to imaginary companions. All this made those who saw her think she must be out of her mind.[1]

But Elizabeth Van Lew was not crazy. She knew what she was doing. By herself, or with members of her family, she acted like a completely sane person. They knew she was very intelligent.

Crazy Bet was putting on an act. Her purpose was to make the people of Richmond believe she could not plan anything against them. Actually, she planned many things against them, and her plans worked.

Richmond was a city at war. It became the capital of the Southern Confederacy after the outbreak of the Civil War in 1861. Jefferson Davis became president of the Confederacy. He led a government that intended to separate the southern states from the Union of the United States.

Armies maneuvered in and around Richmond. Soldiers in uniform marched through the streets. Wounded men from the battlefields flooded into Richmond and filled the hospitals. Women served as nurses. Men built defenses in case the enemy attacked the city. Everyone lived in fear of what might happen.

Van Lew lived through this turmoil. She had been in Richmond all her life. She would not leave because of the Civil War. The interesting thing is that she supported the North. She stood for the Union, and she did it in Richmond, the heart of the Confederacy.

She was a spy for the Union. If that fact had been known in Richmond, she could have been executed as a spy. To avoid suspicion, she acted the part of Crazy Bet. Nobody took her seriously. That was her secret. As she wrote about her odd behavior: "This helps me in my work."[2]

Elizabeth Van Lew was born in Richmond, Virginia, on October 15, 1818. Her father was a well-to-do hardware merchant. Her mother belonged to an upper-class Virginia family. Both of her parents loved books, and she learned to love reading in their library. This shows in her diary, which is well written and mentions good books she read.

After Elizabeth's father's death, her mother freed their own slaves as a part of an antislavery effort. In 1859, just before the Civil War, the Van Lews defended John Brown when he seized a United States arsenal at Harpers Ferry, Virginia. Brown's purpose was to start a slave revolt. He failed and was captured and executed. Van Lew condemned Brown's resort to violence, but she insisted that Brown was right about slavery. She believed it had to be ended.[3]

After the Civil War began, the South won the Battle of Bull Run on July 21, 1861. Many Confederate wounded came into Richmond from the battlefield, which was only about thirty miles away. Van Lew was among the women who cared for them. She also volunteered to care for the Union wounded.

Some Union soldiers were captured at Bull Run. They were held in a Richmond prison. Van Lew brought food and books to them. This caused her to be criticized by the Confederates, but they allowed her to do it. They thought Crazy Bet was harmless.

She smuggled messages into the prison, telling prisoners what was happening outside the prison walls. She encouraged them to hope for a Union victory. She kept her diary at the same time, setting down her thoughts about the Civil War. She wrote about seven hundred pages, of which four hundred survived the war.[4] Hers is often the best account we have of Richmond at the time.

Van Lew started her diary with a few simple words: "1861. The beginning of the war."[5] Her description of war fever in the Confederacy was: "The whole South became one great military school."[6] She meant that nearly everybody in the South wanted to go to war against the North. She kept on writing throughout the Civil War years of 1861 to 1865.

A spy herself, she used servants and friends as secret agents. They sneaked through battle lines to report to Union officers. She aided Union spies who sneaked into Richmond. She used her own house as a safe place where they could hide in Richmond.

Van Lew's reports about the Confederacy were so accurate that Union generals began to rely on them. She told the generals about the fighting ability of the Confederate army. She told them about Confederate plans to use that army. Knowing these facts permitted the Union generals to prepare for battle.

In 1863, General Benjamin Butler sent a secret agent into Richmond, asking Van Lew to spy for him.[7] Butler commanded the Union army on the James River. Richmond was on the James River. Therefore, Butler's headquarters were close enough for Van Lew's secret agents to meet him quickly. He could tell her what he wanted to know. She could tell him what she knew.

Butler suggested that she use "Babcock" as a secret name in writing to him. She did, until a real man named Babcock was arrested. Then "Romona" became her secret name. She called herself "Romona" until the end of the Civil War.

Van Lew's spy activities extended throughout Richmond. She even placed a secret agent in the home of Jefferson Davis, president of the Confederacy.[8] Mr. and Mrs. Davis needed a servant. Van Lew sent them Mary Bowser, who agreed to spy for her in the Davis home. Bowser heard secrets that Davis discussed with his generals. She slipped out at night to report to Van Lew on a farm outside Richmond.

Van Lew played the part of Crazy Bet. She wore ragged clothing. She talked to herself. She drove through Richmond in a battered horse and wagon. Nobody stopped her.

Bowser took military plans from the Davis house to Van Lew, who sent them on to General Butler.

In 1864, General Ulysses S. Grant was in command of the Union army. His plan was to drive back the Confederate forces under General Robert E. Lee and take Richmond. Grant wanted to know how Lee was organizing his defenses.

Van Lew provided this information. She sent a secret agent to General Butler, warning that Lee was massing his troops south of Richmond.[9] Butler reported this to Grant, who moved his Union troops south to challenge Lee. This led to a series of battles in which Grant defeated Lee.

Elizabeth Van Lew's information helped Ulysses S. Grant in a series of crucial battles.

In visiting the main prison in Richmond, Van Lew learned that a group of prisoners was planning to escape. They were digging a secret tunnel through which they might crawl to freedom. Van Lew informed Butler and urged him to send a raiding party to enter Richmond and rescue the prisoners.

The plan failed because the James River was too high to cross. The Union raiding party was driven off by the Confederates. However, a lot of prisoners escaped. Some hid in Van Lew's house in Richmond and got away.

Grant's soldiers captured Richmond. When he rode into the city, he stopped to meet Van Lew. He thanked her for all the information she had given him.[10]

The Civil War ended with Lee's surrender to Grant at Appomattox Court House on April 9, 1865. A number of Union officers remembered Van Lew's contribution to the victory. General Butler said that Van Lew "was my secret correspondent in Richmond."[11] General George Sharpe, the head of Grant's spy department, said: "For a long, long time she represented all that was left of the power of the United States in the city of Richmond."[12] No higher praise was given to any other spy of the Civil War.

After the Civil War, Van Lew celebrated the Union victory. Then she found herself in difficulties. She spent most of her money on her spy activities during the Civil War. Many of her secret agents had to pay for food and transportation, especially horses, when traveling long distances. She was rich enough to pay for them, which she willingly did. The cost of four years of war was too much. Her funds ran out.

Van Lew could not find a job in Richmond. The people of the city saw her welcome the Union army. They realized they had been wrong about Crazy Bet. She had fooled them. She really did spy on them. They refused to be friendly with her, much less give her a job.

Van Lew wrote for help to Unionists in the North. She complained that she was poor because she spent everything on her spy campaign on their behalf. One letter reached Ulysses S. Grant, who was no longer a general. He was the president of the United States. He remembered Van Lew and repaid her by appointing her to run the United States post office in Richmond.

The people there resented her appointment. One newspaper, the *Richmond Dispatch*, wrote on March 23, 1869: "We regard the selection of a Federal spy to manage our post office as a deliberate insult to our people."[13]

Grant saw to it that Van Lew held the post office job in Richmond as long as he was president. She then spent two years in the Washington post office, then returned to Richmond. She preferred to live in her city no matter how many of her neighbors disliked her for her plots against them during the Civil War.

Van Lew again had money troubles. Again she wrote to admirers in the North. Many sent money to her when they learned she was poor again. This income enabled her to pay her way until her death on September 25, 1900.

Belle Boyd

6

Belle Boyd

Stonewall Jackson's Spy

Belle Boyd's real name was Isabelle Boyd. She preferred the shorter form and called herself Belle Boyd. She was an attractive young lady who lived amid the charms of her native Virginia before the Civil War. She saw magnolia trees blossoming, honeysuckle at the doorway, and tobacco plants in the fields. She went on raccoon hunts through the woods on moonlit nights.

In the house, she took part in parties and dances. While well-to-do white people like Belle Boyd enjoyed themselves, slaves did the work. Boyd took slavery for granted because it was part of the society she lived in. This made it easy for her to support the South in its defense of slavery when the Civil War came.

By then she was an expert horsewoman. Horses at that time were what automobiles are today. They were the fastest way to move on the ground. Armies maneuvered across wide-open spaces. Military commanders needed fast communications to keep in touch with one another. Much of the time this could only be done with messengers on horseback.

Boyd acted as a messenger. She was always ready to leap into the saddle and carry messages from one military commander to another. She owned a favorite horse, which she called Fleeter. The word "fleet" means "fast," and the name meant that Fleeter was the fastest horse she rode. It obeyed her slightest touch on the reins. She was able to ride around enemy patrols or outrun them if they spotted her.[1]

Boyd rode Fleeter across Civil War battlefields for many miles and many hours. She was so good that Confederate officers promoted her from being merely a messenger. She became a spy, a teenage spy for the South against the North.

Belle Boyd was born in Martinsburg, Virginia, on May 9, 1844. Martinsburg was in the western part of the state, an area disputed by North and South during the Civil War. After the surrender of the Confederacy, Martinsburg ended up in the new state of West Virginia. The new state was made up of the Virginia counties that remained loyal to the Union during the Civil War.

Martinsburg was held sometimes by Confederate soldiers and sometimes by Union soldiers. Boyd met commanders on both sides, and made friends on both sides. She could get information from Union officers who did not know she was a spy. She could pass the information along to Confederate officers who knew she was a spy, on their side.

Her father, Benjamin Boyd, kept a big store. Her mother, Mary Glenn Boyd, was the daughter of an officer in the United States Army. The family never wavered in its support for the Confederacy against the Union.

When the Confederacy declared its independence in 1861 and the Civil War began, men all over the South rushed to volunteer in the Confederate army. Boyd's father joined the second regiment of the First Virginia Brigade. This became known as the Stonewall Brigade, named for Stonewall Jackson. Boyd's daughter, Belle, would serve as a spy for Jackson.[2]

At twelve, Belle Boyd went to Mount Washington Female College in Baltimore. She learned English literature and French before returning home with her diploma. The clash between the North and South was getting worse. The outcome was the Civil War in 1861. Boyd was in Martinsburg when the break came. After that, she lived part of the time in her aunt's house in Front Royal, where much of her spying would be done.

Boyd was for the rebellion. She saw herself as "a rebel lady."[3]

One of Boyd's friends was Turner Ashby, a cavalry commander who ran the Confederate spy network. Knowing she could ride through Union lines, Ashby asked her to become a spy for him. Battle lines were fluid, with big gaps between military units. Boyd could avoid capture as she rode through the gaps. She could report to Ashby or to the first Confederate officer she met. She agreed to do it.

Boyd rode many short rides. When she could not go herself, she sent messengers. One was Eliza Hopewell, a Boyd servant.[4] Hopewell was successful because most slaves were not suspected by Union officers. Most of these officers could not believe that slave women would be trusted with important messages. In fact, these women were among the smartest spies of the Civil War.

When Union forces took over Front Royal, the military commanders held a conference in the Boyd house. Boyd listened through a hole in an upstairs room and heard what they were planning.

Boyd sneaked out of the house in the darkness, saddled her horse, and rode through the Union lines to the Confederate lines. She met Ashby and told him about the Union conference she had overheard. Then she rode back and was in her room in Front Royal before daybreak. The Union forces never guessed she had been away. They never knew that her spying allowed the Confederates to shift their own forces to confront the Union forces.[5]

Stonewall Jackson launched his attack on Front Royal. The Union forces hastily began a retreat. The people in the town saw complete confusion in their streets as men rushed to get away before Jackson trapped them. They hauled guns and supplies away to prevent the Confederates from seizing anything of use to their troops.

Boyd saw panicky Unionists running past her house. She rushed to a balcony and trained opera glasses on the whole area. She saw that only a few Union soldiers remained in Front Royal. She resolved to get this vital information to Jackson.

Some men were standing outside her house. Boyd told them that she had an important warning for Stonewall Jackson. She hoped that one of them would volunteer. All refused. The response she received from them was: "No, no! You go!"[6]

She did. She set out on foot, running as fast as she could through Front Royal and into the country-side. This time it was not just a matter of sneaking through enemy lines unobserved. Confederates and Unionists were firing at one another, and the direction she had to take was in between them. She later wrote that bullets whizzed around her and tore through her clothing. At one point, she threw herself on the ground as a shell exploded. The fragments of the shell flew harmlessly over her head. Regaining her feet, she raced toward the Confederate line.

Boyd ran into a friend on Jackson's staff, who reported to the general that a teenage girl had a warning for him about the Unionists in Front Royal. She said that a quick calvary charge could catch all of the enemy still there. Stonewall Jackson acted on her warning. His calvary charged forward and captured Front Royal.[7]

What Boyd says about this incident has been contradicted by some who consider it a made-up story. It may be that her memory failed her on some details. Yet, the truth of her warning to Stonewall Jackson is supported by Jackson himself. Right after the battle on May 23, 1862, he wrote to her: "Miss Belle Boyd, I thank you for myself and for the Army, for the immense service that you have rendered your country today."[8]

Union officers had seen Boyd run to Jackson's headquarters at Front Royal. They knew she was a spy for the Confederates. As a result, they arrested her when they found her after they captured Front Royal.

Boyd was taken to Washington and put into prison. She refused to hide her Confederate sympathies. One thing she did was to sing "Maryland, My Maryland" so loudly that most of the other prisoners in their cells could hear her. This song was sung by Marylanders who backed the Confederacy.

The chief of espionage in Washington, Lafayette Baker, questioned Boyd harshly. The evidence that she was a spy was so strong that she could have been "shot at sunrise," as poet Carl Sandburg said.[9] But to execute an eighteen-year-old girl was unthinkable.

General Thomas J. "Stonewall" Jackson

Baker ordered Boyd to be sent back to the Confederacy. She went to Martinsburg, and was there when Union forces again occupied the town. They arrested her again, and again told her to stay in the Confederacy. This time she stayed.

Boyd did not stop working for the Confederacy. She agreed to go to London in hope of winning English support that might force the Union to a compromise peace. Still a spy, she used the secret name "Mrs. Lewis" while abroad.[10] She believed she was as likely to succeed as any man would on a spy mission. She wrote: "Women can sometimes work wonders."[11]

Her expectations were too high. She got nothing from the London government. With despair, she learned of the surrender of Robert E. Lee to Ulysses S. Grant at Appomattox Court House on April 9, 1865. The Confederacy came to an end, and her spying for the Confederacy came to an end.

Boyd struck one last blow for the lost cause when she wrote her book *Belle Boyd in Camp and Prison*. Published in London in 1865, the book made her a heroine to some of her readers. They considered her a gallant lady who suffered for her loyalty to the Confederacy during the Civil War. Other readers condemned her defense of rebellion and slavery.

Boyd had to remain in London because rebels were barred from the United States. Then President Andrew Johnson forgave all former rebels. She could go home, which she did. She went on the stage as an actress, performing across America. She was a good actress, even playing the part of Juliet in Shakespeare's *Romeo and Juliet.*

Having married three times during her fifty-six years, she left five grown children when she died on June 11, 1900.

Allan Pinkerton

Allan Pinkerton

Spy and Spymaster

Abraham Lincoln was elected president of the United States on November 6, 1860. He stood for maintaining the Union of all the states. He was also for preventing the extension of slavery beyond the states where it already existed.

On both these points, he was opposed by the Southern states. Southerners defended their right to secede from the Union. By "secede" they meant that they would break away from the Union and set up an independent nation of their own. They intended to preserve slavery in their new nation.

The first threat of the South was to prevent Lincoln from becoming president. He had to travel by railroad from Springfield, Illinois, to Washington, D.C. There would be stops at Philadelphia and

Baltimore. He might be assassinated in either of these cities.

The head of the railroad called in Allan Pinkerton to investigate. Pinkerton was the director of a detective agency in Chicago. He had solved many crimes. He agreed to travel on the railroad and see where Lincoln faced real danger. His report, after the trip, stated that "bitter and violent" men were planning to assassinate the President.[1]

Pinkerton sent his detectives to stops along the railroad line. Their orders were to investigate the "bitter and violent" men. The detectives were at their posts when Lincoln's trains rolled eastward from Illinois toward Washington. At Philadelphia, Pinkerton met Lincoln. The detective from Chicago joined the president's party on a train for Baltimore. Then, they changed trains and continued safely to Washington.

Pinkerton could claim that he escorted Lincoln safely to the White House despite the dangers along the way. Recognizing Pinkerton's ability in handling undercover cases, Lincoln asked him to set up a secret service in Washington. Pinkerton agreed. Pinkerton the detective became a spy because he carried out espionage missions himself. He became a spymaster because he ran a group of spies.

Allan Pinkerton was born on August 25, 1819, in Glasgow, Scotland. His father was a blacksmith. His mother worked in a mill, where she spun thread into men's and women's clothing. The Pinkerton family was poor, and Allan had to leave school to work in a factory.

Ten years later, he became a cooper, or maker of wooden barrels. He became involved in political rioting, which made it impossible for him to remain in Scotland. He married Joan Carfrae in 1842, and they moved across the Atlantic to Chicago. He detected a gang of criminals who made counterfeit money, and reported them to the police. The Chicago authorities offered him a job in law enforcement. That was how Pinkerton became a detective.[2]

In 1850, he opened his own detective agency. He hired the best men he could find to be his detectives. Under his leadership, they solved many crimes across the country. Pinkerton's detectives were known as Pinkertons, a name that became famous.

Some of the worst crimes were committed against the railroads.[3] Gangs raided railroad cars carrying gold and jewelry. They robbed construction sites where railroad tracks and railroad stations were being built. They murdered railroad workers who tried to stop them. One murder of a superintendent on the Central Illinois Railroad was so brutal that the officers of the railroad appealed to Pinkerton for help.

Pinkerton assigned his detectives to the Central Illinois case. They were so successful in catching criminals that crimes along the railroad lines were greatly reduced. Other railroad officers got to know Pinkerton as the one who could solve their crime problems. They went to him for help.[4]

Pinkerton and his detectives knew how to protect railroads. Naturally, they got the job of protecting President Lincoln on his railroad journey to Washington. When Pinkerton became a spymaster in Washington, he took his detectives with him. They were his spies.

Pinkerton's first espionage assignment was with General George McClellan, who held a command in Ohio. They were old friends, for McClellan had been a director of the Central Illinois Railroad when Pinkerton worked for it. When McClellan was ordered to Washington, Pinkerton went with him. McClellan took command of the Army of the Potomac. Pinkerton established an espionage system. His duties were to send Union spies into the South, and to catch Confederate spies in the North.[5] He used the secret name "E. J. Allen."

The Union army lost the Battle of Bull Run to the Confederate army on July 21, 1861. There was fear in Washington that the national capital would be attacked. Pinkerton therefore spied on men and women suspected of spying for the Confederacy. The biggest catch for him and his men was Rose Greenhow, who sent secret messages to Confederate commanders. She helped the Confederates win the Battle of Bull Run. Pinkerton arrested Greenhow, who was forced to leave the Union and stay in the Confederacy.[6]

The most dangerous duty Pinkerton assigned to his spies was to spy in Richmond, the capital of the

Confederacy. He selected only men he trusted. They had to be brave, smart, and willing to put their lives on the line. If captured in Richmond, they could be executed.

Pinkerton's chief spy was Timothy Webster, who had joined the Pinkerton Agency in Chicago. He was one of the Pinkertons who protected the railroad lines as Lincoln rode through to Washington. Webster volunteered to spy in Richmond. When he got there, he pretended to be a supporter of the Confederacy. He posed as a messenger carrying mail between Washington and Richmond. He received permission in both cities. Individuals were allowed to do this as long as they were not suspected of spying.

On his first journey to the South, Webster carried letters from people in Baltimore who had relatives in Richmond. Having delivered the letters in Richmond, he strolled around inspecting the city's defenses. He counted guns that were being installed. He estimated the number of soldiers who manned the defenses.

Then Timothy Webster left Richmond for Washington. He was still pretending that he was simply delivering the mail. He reported everything he knew to Pinkerton, who complimented him on his performance in Richmond. "This first visit of Timothy Webster to Richmond," Pinkerton wrote, "was highly successful."[7]

On his return to Richmond, Webster made friends with persons in high places from whom he

Major Allan Pinkerton (left), President Abraham Lincoln, and
General John A. McClernand at Antietam, in October 1862.

could obtain secret information. Among them was Judah P. Benjamin, the Confederate secretary of war. Webster delivered mail to Benjamin, who gave him passes to travel around the Confederacy. The passes allowed Webster to visit Tennessee, Kentucky, and Virginia. He reported on all of them to Pinkerton in Washington.

In January 1862, Webster paid his last visit to Richmond. To Pinkerton's dismay, Webster suddenly dropped out of sight. When nothing was heard from Webster for some weeks, Pinkerton sent two more spies to look for him. They were Price Lewis and John Scully. They found a tragedy in Richmond.[8]

Lewis and Scully located Webster in a hotel. Webster told them that, after arriving in the Confederate capital, he suffered an attack of rheumatism. It was a painful sickness that forced him to go to a hotel. He hoped to be out of the hotel in a few days and resume his spy mission. However, the rheumatism became worse, and he could not leave the hotel. He could not report to Pinkerton in Washington. That was why weeks went by and Pinkerton heard nothing from Webster in Richmond.

A Confederate army officer grew suspicious of Lewis and Scully. They were taken to jail, where they confessed they were Union spies. By confessing, they received jail sentences instead of being executed.

They named Webster as another Union spy. What they said was fatal to him. The Confederates learned that Webster had come to Richmond secretly to spy on them. He was put on trial, sentenced to death, and hanged on April 30, 1862.[9]

Pinkerton was grief-stricken when he heard the news. Webster had been not only his best spy but also a personal friend. Now, Pinkerton had to go on without him.

The Civil War continued. When McClellan invaded Maryland, Pinkerton went with him to spy on the Confederate army. When McClellan was removed from his command, Pinkerton left military service, too. Pinkerton spent the rest of the Civil War investigating dishonest businessmen doing business with the government.[10] When the Civil War ended in 1865, Pinkerton retired from government work in Washington. He ceased to be a spy and retired to private life in Chicago.

However, even after retirement the spymaster still had influence. Pinkerton ordered his detectives into the investigation of crimes after the Civil War. Gangs armed with pistols and riding horses began robbing banks and trains. The first gang was the Reno gang of Indiana. Pinkerton led a band of lawmen who broke up the Reno gang.[11]

The worst gang was led by Jesse and Frank James. The James boys committed robbery and murder from Missouri to Minnesota. Pinkerton was called in to deal with this gang. Pinkerton said that the James boys and those who followed them were "desperate men" who would stop at nothing.[12] Pinkerton failed to capture the James boys. Jesse James got away, only to be shot by a member of his own gang. Frank James surrendered to the governor of Missouri.

Pinkerton's biggest criminal case came with the Molly Maguires, a secret society in the coal mines of Pennsylvania. The Molly Maguires terrorized coal miners who opposed them. Pinkerton selected a detective especially to deal with the secret society. The detective's name was James McParlon. He pretended to join the Molly Maguires, but actually he was a secret agent gathering evidence against them. McParlon was a witness in court in 1876 when some of its members were sentenced to death for murder.[13] Pinkerton continued to be a crime fighter until his death on July 1, 1884. He left behind a great crime-fighting organization that exists to this day, the Pinkertons.

General Mark Clark

Mark Clark

American Spy in North Africa

American General Mark Clark arrived in Gibraltar, in the middle of World War II. Clark was on a special assignment that required him to leave Gibraltar, cross the Mediterranean, and go ashore on the coast of North Africa. At that time, the area was French North Africa, for the French had colonized Algeria and Morocco during the nineteenth century.

In World War II, Germany conquered France. French North Africa fell under German control. America and Britain, the Allies, were planning to invade Algeria and Morocco, and then attack the German forces stationed there. The big question was how the French forces in North Africa would respond to the Allied invasion. Would the French submit to their German conquerors? Or would the French join the Allies in a fight for freedom?[1]

Clark's assignment was to find out. He flew from Britain to Gibraltar, a towering rock on the Mediterranean shore next to Spain. The British owned Gibraltar, which they had turned into a military fortress. The British army, navy, and air force units defended Gibraltar.

A British submarine, the *Seraph*, was in the harbor waiting for Clark and the advisers who traveled with him. He boarded the *Seraph*, and it moved out into the Mediterranean bound for North Africa.

Submarines were small during World War II. Clark was a tall man, six feet two. He found it difficult to move around in the *Seraph*. He could hardly stand up without hitting his head. "I had literally to crawl on all fours," he wrote in his story of his time aboard the submarine.[2]

The *Seraph* crossed the Mediterranean from Gibraltar to Algeria. Clark prepared to go ashore. He had to be careful. He was not just an American general on a military assignment. He was an American spy on an undercover operation.

Mark Clark was born on May 1, 1896, in Watertown, New York. His father, Charles Clark, was a career officer in the United States Army. His mother, Rebecca Ezekiels Clark, was a daughter of Jewish immigrants who came to America hoping for a better life than they had in Europe. Her father found success in the West by becoming a member of the Montana state legislature.

Mark Clark and his sister, Janet, moved frequently because their father, as a soldier, was transferred from one army post to another. After Mark's schooling, he followed his father into West Point and into the United States Army. He rose through the military ranks from lieutenant to general. He served with the infantry in World War I, when he took part in battles against the Germans. He was in action at Saint-Mihiel and the Meuse-Argonne, two American victories that helped the Allies win World War I in 1918.

After the war, Clark held a number of army positions at home from New York to California. He mastered the technique of commanding ground troops in battle.

With this military training, Clark was ready for a fighting command when World War II broke out in 1939. He became a brigadier general (1941), a major general (1942), and a lieutenant general (1942). He was ordered to England to serve under Dwight D. Eisenhower's command. The Allies intended to invade France and attack the Germans there. The Allies would have to cross the English Channel, an enormous operation. They did not have enough trained men. They did not have enough tanks or planes. They needed time to plan the invasion of France. This invasion would not take place until D-Day, June 6, 1944.

Meanwhile, in 1942, North Africa could be invaded. Eisenhower was going to send his troops into Algeria and Morocco. The French commander in North Africa was General Charles Mast. Mast sent a secret message to Eisenhower, saying he would reveal his intentions to an American spy. The spy would have to come to a secret meeting in Algeria. Mast added that the American spy must be a high-ranking American general. Eisenhower chose Clark.[3]

And so, Clark traveled by submarine from Gibraltar to Algeria. When the *Seraph* left deep Mediterranean water and surfaced near the Algerian shore, it was night. A signal light gleaming through the darkness told Clark and his party that they could safely come ashore. The signal was a lamp in the window of a farmhouse.[4]

Clark and his advisers scrambled off the submarine into small boats that rode big waves into the shore. The Americans waded through the surf. They hurried inland guided by the light in the farmhouse window. They were greeted by the French farmer, who informed them that General Mast was on his way. When Mast arrived, it was October 21, 1942. He was accompanied by officers of his staff. The two groups, American and French, began their secret spy meeting. The French general said he would cooperate with the American invasion of North Africa.

The American forces were to land near the two big cities of Algiers and Casablanca. American planes would bomb the Germans. American paratroopers would land behind the German lines. Mast gave Clark all the information he had about the situation in North Africa. The French general noted how strong the Germans and their French supporters were. He suggested the best way for the Americans to attack them was by land and by air. He promised his own army would join the Americans.[5]

Mast went back to Algiers, leaving his officers to continue the meeting with Clark. The phone rang. The farmer answered. Suddenly he shouted: "The police will be here in a few minutes!"[6] The police supported the Germans in North Africa. They suspected that anti-German activities were going on in the farmhouse. They were racing toward the farmhouse in the hope of capturing anti-German conspirators.

There was not a moment to lose. Clark and his men had to hide before the police arrived. The farmer pulled open a secret trapdoor in the floor of the farmhouse. The Americans dropped through the trapdoor into the room below and found themselves in a wine cellar. The trapdoor closed over their heads. They crouched down in the pitch darkness of the wine cellar. They could hear the police arrive and search the farmhouse. Clark feared that the police might find the trapdoor and corner the Americans in the wine cellar. He and his men were armed. They were ready to shoot their way out. Clark warned them not to shoot too soon. "I whispered that no one was to fire unless I did."[7]

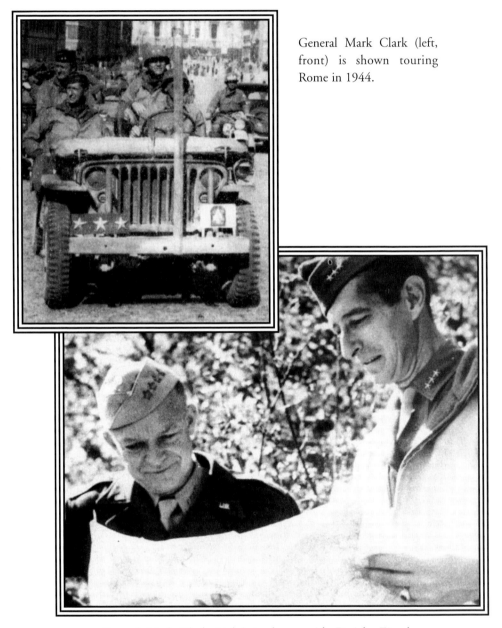

General Mark Clark (left, front) is shown touring Rome in 1944.

General Mark Clark (right) is shown with Dwight Eisenhower, supreme commander of the Allied Expeditionary Force in Europe. Clark acquired information that was vital to the success of the 1942 Allied invasion of North Africa and eventually the D-Day invasion on June 6, 1944.

Fortunately, the police walked back and forth over the trapdoor but never discovered it. They went away. The Americans climbed out of the wine cellar and ran to the beach where their boats were hidden. The waves were so high that it took several attempts before they could get their boats through the waves. At last the Americans made it back to the submarine, which was waiting for them.[8]

They traveled from Algeria to Gibraltar. Clark wrote a report on the secret spy meeting. The report was sent to military headquarters "for Eisenhower's eyes only."[9] Clark assured Eisenhower that the Americans would have French support when they fought their way into North Africa. Clark was a successful spy. As a British historian wrote: "The Americans had arranged contact with [patriotic Frenchmen] through General Mark Clark, who landed from a British submarine at Cherchell, ninety miles from Algiers, on 21 October."[10]

World War II went on for another three years, from 1942 to 1945. Clark took part in the fighting from the invasion of North Africa to the invasion of Italy. He commanded Allied forces that defeated the Germans in Italy in 1945. His next fighting command was in the Pacific, in the Korean War. This war ended when he signed an agreement with the North Koreans and the Chinese on July 27, 1953.

Mark Clark then retired from the military and returned home. He was appointed president of The Citadel, the Military College of South Carolina, on

March 19, 1954. This position let him use his military experience in educating future officers of the United States Army. The Citadel in Charleston, South Carolina was known as "the West Point of the South," but it was suffering from neglect. Discipline was lax among the cadets. Some professors were not up to par. Too many buildings were run down.

Clark changed all this. He enjoyed the respect of everyone at The Citadel because of his distinguished career in the army. He ordered the cadets to obey strict discipline, stressing soldierly salute when spoken to by their superior officers. He brought in professors of the highest ability. He built new buildings, especially scientific laboratories. He insisted that everyone practice the honor system, by which they pledged always to tell the truth.[11]

Clark admired the people of Charleston because they believed in Americanism. As he said: "Charleston believes in the military, believes in being strong, believes in national defense."[12] He was popular in Charleston, addressing large audiences when he spoke on national and international problems.

Clark and his first wife, Maurine Doran, were popular with the cadets, whom they often entertained in their home. They had a daughter, and a son who followed him into the army. After Maurine's death in 1966, he married Mary Applegate.

When Clark retired from The Citadel on June 30, 1969, he left a vastly improved institution to his successor. He died on April 17, 1984.

Josephine Baker
American Spy in France

Josephine Baker of St. Louis, Missouri, used to stroll down the streets of Paris with a leopard on a leash. Her leopard was only half-grown. Nevertheless, it was a dangerous animal. A leopard is a big cat, in the same class with lions and tigers. So, the people of Paris noticed Baker, and made her famous as the lady with the leopard. They did not want to get too close when Baker walked past with her big cat. At the same time, they stopped to watch. They were fascinated by the sight.[1]

Baker put a collar covered with diamonds around her leopard's neck. She could afford diamonds because she was a star of the Paris theater. She was paid enormous sums to perform on stage.

Josephine Baker

Her appearances on stage were spectacular. She wore colorful costumes made of silk and satin. These costumes sparkled in brilliant jewels. Her necklace was of large gleaming pearls. She wore peacock feathers in her hair. She waved big fans made of ostrich feathers.

Nearly every Paris audience cheered Baker when she performed at the theater. She charmed them with songs in English and French. She danced the American Charleston. She danced to the latest French music. She knew how to entertain an audience as well as any performer of her time.

Her leopard grew up, and had to be sent to the zoo. She remained a star without it. Everyone in Paris wanted to meet Josephine Baker, the actress. She had hundreds of friends in all walks of life. Her fame extended across Europe and America.

As the year 1939 began, Baker was simply an American actress in Paris. As 1939 ended, she was an American spy in Paris.

Josephine Baker was born on June 3, 1906, in St. Louis, Missouri. She was an African American. Her mother, Carrie McDonald, worked as a servant in white households. Her father, Eddie Carson, played drums on riverboats sailing along the Mississippi River. Sometimes they performed together, for Carrie was a singer. When Josephine was a baby, they took her with them onto the stage.[2]

The family was poor. As a child, Josephine used to knock on doors asking for work. If lucky, she was invited to baby-sit or clean house. If unlucky, she had to grab spoiled vegetables in the market or take coal from freight trains standing in the station.

"The day came," she wrote, "when I thought my life had changed for good."[3] She went to live with a white family, for whom she did housekeeping. She also attended school. However, the day came when her job was finished, and she had to leave. Life was hard again until she began to sing and dance in public. She joined an acting company, with which she performed in cities from New Orleans to Chicago and New York. She married Willie Baker, who worked on one of the trains. They did not remain together very long, but she kept her married name and remained Josephine Baker.

She became a star of the American stage. Her big break came when she was invited to appear in Paris. She went, became a star, and decided to stay in France permanently.

Then came 1939, and the outbreak of World War II on September 3. Adolf Hitler's German army invaded Poland. The Allies, France and Britain, declared war on Germany. Nevertheless, hostilities did not begin at once. The two sides faced each other with hardly a shot fired. This period was called the "phony war."

Baker became a spy during the phony war. The French secret service needed undercover agents who could move around without being suspected. Baker could do this in Paris. An officer of the secret service named Jacques Abtey came to her with a special request. Italy had not joined Germany in World War II. Baker agreed to investigate, for she was welcome at the Italian Embassy in Paris.[4]

Baker went to the Italian embassy many times. She talked to men and women who worked there and listened to their conversation about the war. She reported to Abtey what she learned. He said her reports contained extremely useful information. Baker could not inform him whether Mussolini would attack France (later on, he did). Still, Baker proved she could be a successful spy.[5]

On May 10, 1940, the phony war turned into a real war. The German armed forces invaded France with infantry, tanks, and planes. Thousands of French refugees fled from this devastating attack. They walked, rode bicycles, and rolled away in cars and buses.

Baker was one of the refugees. She was tending to French soldiers in the hospitals when Abtey warned her to leave Paris. She took his advice. She gathered as many of her belongings as she could. She rolled off in her car, joining the thousands fleeing to the south of France.

The French surrendered. The Germans divided France into two parts. One part was occupied France, controlled by the Germans in Paris. The other part was unoccupied France, ruled by Marshal Henri Philippe Pétain, who set up his government in the city of Vichy. It seemed that the French people

Josephine Baker witnessed firsthand the tragedy of the German occupation of France. This Frenchman sobs at the news of the German occupation.

would be governed either by the Germans in Paris or by Pétain in Vichy.

But, they could listen to General Charles de Gaulle, who had escaped to London. De Gaulle spoke to the French people by radio. He urged them to resist both the Germans and Pétain. He promised that they would one day be free.

Baker heard de Gaulle's radio speeches. She believed him and became an enemy of both the

Germans in Paris and Pétain in Vichy. She looked forward to the day when de Gaulle would return to a liberated France.[6]

There was spying to be done. Freedom fighters in France were in communication with General de Gaulle in London. De Gaulle sent them orders by radio about waging an undercover battle against the Germans in France. The freedom fighters in France sent de Gaulle reports about how the battle was going. Throughout France, men and women volunteered to spy for de Gaulle.

These spies operated under the noses of the Germans in occupied France. The spies operated in unoccupied France, defying Marshal Pétain. The French surrender to the Germans in 1940 included the surrender of French North Africa, meaning Algeria and Morocco.

Baker volunteered to spy for de Gaulle and the French freedom fighters wherever they wanted her to go. Being a singer enabled her to move around without being suspected of espionage. Wherever she happened to be, she performed in the theater. After the performance, she talked with members of the audience who came to see her. This included Germans in the audience. Any information that could help de Gaulle, she reported to freedom fighters she met secretly.

One assignment took her to Lisbon, Portugal, where a spy might hear gossip about what the Germans were doing. She learned some of their secrets. She wrote what she learned on sheets of the music she sang.[7] One thing she learned in Lisbon was the movement of German troops in France. With this knowledge, freedom fighters could attack where there were few Germans and avoid places where the Germans were strong.

Baker spent much of her time in French North Africa reporting from Casablanca in Morocco. She was in Casablanca in 1942 when the American invasion of North Africa took place. She ran onto a balcony to see the Americans occupy Casablanca. "That's the Americans for you," she shouted. "They'll win the war for us!"[8]

When the Germans surrendered in North Africa, Baker toured American and British army camps, singing and dancing for the troops. World War II ended with the German surrender to the Allies on May 8, 1945. Baker returned to liberated France. She was no longer a spy, but the French remembered that she had been a spy during World War II. They gave her two medals for her bravery. General de Gaulle, now president of France, sent her a letter expressing his thanks to her.[9]

Baker resumed her stage career by singing and dancing before enthusiastic audiences.

Although she married four times, she had no children. Therefore, she adopted children. There were a dozen in her home. They were of different races and nationalities, from Europe, Africa, and

Asia. They lived with her quite happily because she believed in racial equality.[10]

Baker took her show on tours outside France. She went to Mexico, Argentina, Italy, Denmark, and Israel. Her American tours were the most important to her because she was able to strike a blow against racism. From New York in the East to Los Angeles on the West Coast, she insisted that her audiences be integrated. This was a brave thing to do in the days when segregation was common in American theaters and restaurants.

In 1973, she had her biggest success in America. She performed in New York's Carnegie Hall. Actors and actresses are proud to say they have appeared once onstage in Carnegie Hall. Baker appeared four times. Each time, she was cheered and applauded.

Of course, she demanded that her audiences be integrated. Times were changing in America. Baker supported the civil rights movement of the 1960s. She was pleased to see racial barriers come down. She enjoyed the compliments she received for her efforts on behalf of civil rights.

Baker's last years were unhappy. She was getting old and sick. She was deeply in debt. Her house outside Paris was sold to pay those to whom she owed money. She depended on gifts from her friends.

One thing could not be taken from Josephine Baker: her memories of her great days as an actress and a spy. She still had those memories on the day of her death, April 14, 1975.

Moe Berg

Moe Berg

Baseball's Spy

In 1934, a team of American baseball players arrived in Tokyo. They were all-stars, some of the best players in the National League and the American League. Babe Ruth was the captain of the team that also included Lou Gehrig, Jimmy Foxx, and Lefty Grove. Their names were known to baseball fans everywhere.[1]

Baseball was becoming popular in Japan in 1934. Japanese players were eager to play against the best Americans. That was why the American all-stars were in Japan. They played games against the best Japanese players. Some of these Japanese players became known in the United States. That set the stage for the time when Japanese stars would come to

America to play with the Boston Red Sox, the St. Louis Cardinals, and other American teams.

One player on the 1934 trip to Japan was Moe Berg, a catcher with the Boston Red Sox. Berg was a student of the game. He showed Japanese catchers how to handle pitchers. He showed them how to throw out a runner at second base. He showed them how to block home plate against a runner trying to score from third base.

Berg was an important player in the all-star American lineup. Yet, he failed to show up for one of the big games. His teammates were amazed when he rejoined the team because he refused to tell them where he had been.

He concealed the fact that he had walked through Tokyo snapping pictures with his camera. From the top of a tall building, he could see the city laid out below. He photographed Japanese army barracks, oil refineries, and factories. He swung his camera around and snapped pictures of Tokyo harbor, where warships were anchored.[2] Berg concentrated on military installations because he was not just an American baseball player in Japan. He was a spy for the American government.

Moe Berg was born on March 2, 1902, in New York. His first name was Morris, but he was always called Moe. His parents came from Russia, hoping for a better life in America. They found it when his father became a druggist. Moe and his brother received a good education in high school.

Moe also played baseball in high school. He continued with the game when he went to college. He played shortstop for the Princeton team that won nineteen games in a row.[3]

Berg was an excellent student. He learned Latin, Greek, German, Italian, Japanese, and Spanish. After graduation, he might have become a professor. Instead he went into baseball, joining the Brooklyn Dodgers as a shortstop. He was a good fielder and formed a good double-play combination with the second baseman.

Two years later he was traded to the Chicago White Sox. Here he became a catcher, his best position. He also played catcher when he was traded to the Cleveland Indians. He was good enough to be named to the American all-stars in 1934. He therefore traveled with them to Japan.[4]

There was a second reason for him to play in Japan. He spoke Japanese. This meant that the team headed by Babe Ruth did not need an interpreter in Japan. They had their own interpreter, Moe Berg.

There was a third reason for Berg to play in Japan. He went to Tokyo because Cordell Hull, the secretary of state in Washington, asked him to go. In 1934, the Japanese were threatening to start a war in the Far East. Hull needed a spy in Tokyo. Berg answered the call of his country and patriotically agreed to spy while he was in Japan.[5]

Berg had an excellent cover story. He seemed to be just a baseball player like the other American all-stars. That was what the Japanese thought. Some of the Americans wondered why he was away from the team without explanation. Lefty Grove, the great pitcher for the Philadelphia Athletics, remarked: "Some of the fellows thought Moe was an undercover man for the government . . . He had mysterious meetings and we didn't know what he was doing."[6]

When the American all-stars returned to America, Berg handed in his photographs of Tokyo to the State Department in Washington. Those photographs were used by the American armed forces in planning for war. General James H.

In 1934, Moe Berg (front, right) was a catcher with an all-star American team that played in Tokyo. He was also a spy for the American government.

Doolittle studied Berg's photographs before he led the first American air raid on Tokyo in 1942.[7] They were used in the later air raids that helped win the war in the Pacific.

Berg quit baseball in 1941. On December 7, 1941, the Japanese attacked Pearl Harbor in Hawaii. That attack forced the United States into World War II. Berg was sent on spy assignments overseas. He sneaked into Yugoslavia to report on the Yugoslav civil war. He reported that the Communists were too strong to be defeated. He was right. The Communists seized power in Yugoslavia.[8]

After that, Berg became involved in atomic espionage. In Washington, it was feared that Hitler's scientists would develop an atomic bomb using materials from a factory in Norway. Berg dropped by parachute into Norway.[9] He found that Germans were using the factory. So, the factory was bombed.

Berg carried out more spy missions in Europe. In 1944, he went to Switzerland to attend a lecture by Werner Heisenberg, the foremost German atomic scientist. Berg's mission was to hear what Heisenberg said about the atom. He was to see if Heisenberg mentioned that German scientists were close to making an atomic bomb.

Heisenberg said nothing about the atomic bomb. Berg concluded that the Germans had not figured out how to make an atomic bomb. Berg's report was so important that it was sent to President Roosevelt, who learned that German scientists were far behind

American scientists in atomic research.[10] The
Americans were secretly building the bomb that
would force Japan to surrender.

Berg remained in Switzerland, a neutral country
where spies for Hitler's Germany were operating.
Berg spied on Hitler's spies. Sometimes he used dis-
guises to avoid suspicion. He wore old clothes that
made him look like a refugee. Once, he colored his
hair white to get close to a suspect without being rec-
ognized. He secretly made copies of the suspect's
scientific drawings.[11]

The search for German scientists sped up when
Nazi Germany collapsed. The Americans wanted to
bring the Germans to America, where they would
work in American laboratories. So, there was compe-
tition between the Americans and the Russians to get
to the Germans first.

Berg was one of the Americans who went into
Germany looking for German scientists. He helped
discover one German group that was developing a
secret technique for flying planes faster than the
speed of sound.[12]

Berg did not always get along with other
Americans in espionage. He argued with Allen
Dulles, America's spymaster in Switzerland. Dulles
insisted that Berg report to him. Berg refused. He
said his orders were to report to William Donovan,
head of American espionage. Berg continued to
report to Donovan, not to Dulles.

Nevertheless, Berg and Dulles cooperated on some spy operations. One concerned a German cyclotron, or atom-smashing machine. Berg needed assistance, and he asked Dulles to put more spies on the operation. Dulles did. The plan was to get American spies from Switzerland into Germany before the German surrender. A couple of American spies failed to carry out their assignments. As Berg feared, the Americans were arrested, and the plan failed.[13]

Other operations succeeded. Some were top secret. The truth about them did not come out until years later. Berg must have been very pleased when Werner Heisenberg was captured by the Americans. Heisenberg did not build an atomic bomb. But he was an expert on the theory of the atom, and it was fortunate that he would now be working for the Americans.

With the end of World War II in 1945, Berg went to Denmark to meet Niels Bohr, a Danish atomic scientist. The Americans feared that Bohr might have passed atomic secrets to the Russians. Bohr assured Berg that this was not so. Berg's report caused much relief in Washington.[14]

The Denmark trip was one of Berg's last missions for the U.S. government. On October 19, 1946, he resigned from the spy business.

Berg never boasted about his career. He was a quiet man who did not like to talk about himself. He said little about his time in baseball.

101

This was even more true about his time as a spy. Much of what he did was secret. He could not speak about his espionage missions to Japan, Switzerland, Germany, or Denmark. He swore to keep them secret. He kept his word.[15]

Berg kept up with science. He read books on the atomic bomb. He attended scientific conferences and talked with scientists about their work in the laboratories. He never stopped learning languages.

Baseball remained Berg's favorite sport. He followed the teams and the pennant races. He watched the new stars like Jackie Robinson and Willie Mays. The Red Sox offered Berg a job. He refused the offer. He probably did not want to give up his privacy by working in an office.

He attended baseball games in the big-league cities. He said that "the years with the White Sox were my favorite."[16] New teams came into the big leagues, and he followed them, too. One was the New York Mets. When Berg died on May 30, 1972, his last words were: "How did the Mets do today?"[17]

Chapter Notes

Chapter 1. Nathan Hale: George Washington's Spy

1. Edward Everett Hale, "Captain Nathan Hale," The Connecticut Society of the Sons of the American Revolution, <http://www.ctssar.org/patriots/nathan_hale.htm> (July 14, 2003).

2. Thomas Fleming, *Liberty: The American Revolution* (New York: Viking, 1997), p. 147.

3. Hale.

4. Ralph K. Andrist, ed., *George Washington: A Biography in His Own Words* (New York: Newsweek Books, 1972), pp. 154–156.

5. Hale.

6. Ibid.

7. Ibid.

8. Ibid.

9. Ibid.

10. Fleming, p. 206.

Chapter 2. Benedict Arnold: Patriot, Spy, and Traitor

1. Willard Sterne Randall, *Benedict Arnold: Patriot and Traitor* (New York: William Morrow, 1990), p. 366.

2. Ibid., p. 188.

3. James Thomas Flexner, *The Traitor and the Spy: Benedict Arnold and John André* (Boston, Little Brown, 1975), pp. 230–231.

4. Paul Engle, *Women in the American Revolution* (Chicago: Follett Publishing, 1976), p. 157.

5. Flexner, p. 327.

6. Ralph K. Andrist, ed., *George Washington: A Biography in His Own Words* (New York: Newsweek Books, 1972), pp. 200–201.

7. Ibid., pp. 199–200.

8. Ibid., p. 202.

9. Randall, p. 581.

10. Engle, p. 160.

11. Randall, pp. 612–613.

Chapter 3. Patience Wright: Patriot Spy in London.

1. J. Steven Watson, *The Reign of George III* (Oxford, England: Oxford University Press, 1960), p. 517.

2. Charles Coleman Sellers, *Patience Wright: American Artist and Spy in George III's London* (Middleton, Conn.: Wesleyan University Press, 1976), p. 4.

3. Ibid., pp. 227–233.

4. Paul Engle, *Women in the American Revolution* (Chicago: Follett Publishing, 1976), p. 197.

5. Sellers, p. 56.

6. Philip Thicknesse, *New Prose Bath Guide for the Year 1778 (London and Bath)*. Sellers reprinted, pp. 21–23.

7. Sellers, p. 70.

8. Ibid., p. 82.

9. Ibid., p. 179.

10. Ibid., p. 193.

11. Ibid., p. 84.

Chapter 4. Rose Greenhow: Confederate Spy in Washington

1. Ishbel Ross, *Rebel Rose: Life of Rose O'Neal Greenhow, Confederate Spy* (New York: Harper and Brothers, 1954), p. 72.

2. Michael Farquhar, " 'Rebel Rose,' A Spy of Grande Dame Proportions," September 18, 2000. <http://washingtonpost.com/ac2/wp-dyn?pagename=/article&node=&contentId=A249> (July 14, 2003).

3. Harnett T. Kane, *Spies for the Blue and Gray* (Garden City, N.Y.: Hanover House, 1954), pp. 25–26.

4. Ross, pp. 113–114.

5. Kane, p. 34.

6. Ibid.

7. Ross, pp. 115–116.

8. James D. Horan, *The Pinkertons: The Detective Dynasty That Made History* (New York: Crown Publishers, 1967), pp. 81–98.

9. Ross, p. 234.

10. Ibid., pp. 250–265.

11. Farquhar.

12. Ross, pp. 271–272.

Chapter 5. Elizabeth Van Lew: Union Spy in Richmond

1. Harnett T. Kane, *Spies for the Blue and Gray* (Garden City, N.Y.: Hanover House, 1954), p. 239.

2. Virginius Dabney, *Richmond: The Story of a City* (New York: Doubleday, 1976), p. 181.

3. David D. Ryan, ed., *A Yankee Spy in Richmond: The Civil War Diary of "Crazy Bet" Van Lew* (Mechanicsburg, Pa.: Stackpole Books, 1996), p. 27.

4. Ibid., p. 22.

5. Ibid., p. 27.

6. Ibid., p. 31.

7. Ibid., pp. 51–53.

8. Dabney, p. 180.

9. Ryan, p. 104.

10. Rembert W. Patrick, *The Fall of Richmond* (Baton Rouge: Louisiana State University Press, 1960), p. 76.

11. Ryan, p. 19.

12. Kane, p. 239.

13. Ryan, p. 19.

Chapter 6. Belle Boyd: Stonewall Jackson's Spy

1. Louis A. Sigaud, *Belle Boyd: Confederate Spy* (Richmond: Dietz Press, 1944), pp. 24–25.

2. Curtis Carroll Davis, ed., *Belle Boyd in Camp and Prison, Written by Herself* (Cranbury, N.J.: Thomas Yoseloff, 1968), pp. 124–125.

3. Harnett T. Kane, *Spies for the Blue and Gray* (Garden City, N.Y.: Hanover House, 1954), p. 134.

4. Sigaud, p. 17.

5. Kane, p. 138.

6. Davis, p. 161.

7. Ibid., p. 164.

8. Kane, p. 144.

9. Carl Sandburg, *Abraham Lincoln: The War Years* (New York: Harcourt Brace, 1926), p. 504.

10. Kane, p. 151.

11. Ibid., p. 153.

Chapter 7. Allan Pinkerton: Spy and Spymaster

1. Allan Pinkerton, *The Spy of the Rebellion: Being a True History of the United States Army During the Late Rebellion*, new ed. (Lincoln: University of Nebraska Press, 1989), p. 50.

2. James D. Horan, *The Pinkertons: The Detective Dynasty That Made History* (New York: Crown Publishers, 1967), pp. 16–17.

3. Ibid., p. 32.

4. Ibid., pp. 32–35.

5. Pinkerton, pp. 245–248.

6. Ibid., pp. 250–270.

7. Ibid., p. 325.

8. Ibid., pp. 502–503.

9. Ibid., pp. 557–558.

10. Horan, p. 136.

11. Ibid., p. 171.

12. Ibid., p. 198.

13. Allan Pinkerton, *The Mollie Maguires and the Detectives*, (New York: Haskell House, 1972), p. 505.

Chapter 8. Mark Clark: American Spy in North Africa

1. John Keegan, *The Second World War* (New York: Viking, 1989), p. 340.

2. Mark Clark, *Calculated Risk* (New York: Dodd, Mead, 1970), p. 75.

3. Ibid., p. 68.

4. Ibid., p. 78.

5. Ibid., p. 81.

6. Ibid., p. 82.

7. Ibid., p. 83.

8. Ibid., pp. 86–87.

9. Ibid., pp. 88–89.

10. Keegan, p. 340.

11. Martin Blumenson, *Mark Clark* (New York: Congdon and Weed, 1984), p. 274.

12. Ibid., p. 272.

Chapter 9. Josephine Baker: American Spy in France

1. Lynn Haney, *Naked at the Feast: A Biography of Josephine Baker* (New York: Dodd, Mead, 1981), pp. 162–164.

2. Ibid., p. 9.

3. Josephine Baker and Jo Bouillon, *Josephine* (New York: Harper and Row, 1976), p. 10.

4. Ean Wood, *The Josephine Baker Story* (London: Sanctuary, 2000), p. 213.

5. Ibid., p. 214.

6. Wood, pp. 221–222.

7. Baker and Bouillon, p. 124.

8. Wood, p. 235.

9. Ibid., p. 245.

10. Haney, p. 269.

Chapter 10. Moe Berg: Baseball's Spy

1. Geoffrey C. Ward and Ken Burns, *Baseball: An Illustrated History* (New York: Knopf, 1994), p. 217.

2. Louis Kaufman, Barbara Fitzgerald, and Tom Sewell, *Moe Berg: Athlete, Scholar, Spy* (Boston: Little, Brown, 1974), p. 27.

3. Ibid., p. 48.

4. Ibid., p. 83.

5. Ibid., p. 3.

6. Ibid., p. 122.

7. Ibid., p. 28.

8. Ibid., pp. 161–162.

9. Dan Kurzman, *Blood and Water: Sabotaging Hitler's Bomb* (New York: Henry Holt, 1997), p. 188.

10. Kaufman, Fitzgerald, and Sewell, pp. 195–198.

11. Ibid., p. 200.

12. Ibid., p. 203.

13. Ibid., pp. 203–207.

14. Ibid., pp. 226–227.

15. Ibid., pp. 239–240.

16. Ibid., p. 249.

17. Ibid., p. 264.

Further Reading

Books

Andryzewski, Tricia. *The Amazing Life of Moe Berg: Catcher, Scholar, Spy.* Brookfield, Conn.: Millbrook Press, 1996.

Lough, Loree. *Nathan Hale.* Broomall, Pa.: Chelsea House Publishers, 1999.

Manley, Claudia B. *Secret Agents: Life As a Professional Spy.* New York: Rosen Publishing Group, 2001.

Nofi, Albert A. *Spies in the Civil War.* Broomall, Pa.: Chelsea House Publishers, 1999.

Polmer, Norman, and Thomas B. Allen, *Spy Book: The Encyclopedia of Espionage.* New York: Random House, 1996.

Sullivan, George E. *In the Line of Fire: Eight Women War Spies.* New York: Scholastic, 1996.

Thomas, Paul. *Undercover Agents.* Orlando, Fla.: Raintree Steck-Vaughn, 1998.

Yancey, Diane. *Spies.* Farmington Hills, Mich: Gale Group, 2001.

Zeinert, Karen. *Elizabeth Van Lew: Southern Belle, Union Spy.* Parsippany, N.J.: Dillon Press, 1995.

Ziff, John, *Espionage & Treason.* Broomall, Pa.: Chelsea House Publishers, 2000.

Internet Addresses

Social Studies for Kids

<http://www.socialstudiesforkids.com/wwww/us/
    benedictarnolddef.htm>

**Spy Letters of the American Revolution (From the
Collections of the Clements Library)**

<http://www.si.umich.edu/spies/>

Index